MÁLAGA

Costa del Sol

Torremolinos   Benalmádena   Fuengirola   Mijas
Marbella   Antequera   Ronda   Nerja ......

English Edition

© OTERMIN EDICIONES

Telf.: (+34) 952 29 56 42
Fax.: (+34) 952 20 70 36
Dep. Legal: MA-6542016
ISBN: 84-96298-18-3
www.oterminediciones.com
editorial@oterminediciones.com

Málaga

Panoramic view of Málaga, taken from the Gibralfaro castle

Málaga capital and its province of the same name belong to the autonomous community of Andalusia, in the south of Spain. The city is the second largest of Andalusia in land area and number of inhabitants. The province is bordered to the north by Seville and Córdoba, to the east by Granada, to the west lies Cádiz, and the southern limit is the Mediterranean sea. The area of this province is 7,280 km^2 with 160 km of coastline, reaching from the mouth of the Genal river in the southwest to the bay of Nerja to the east. The predominate climate of Málaga is temperate warm Mediterranean, characterized mainly by a dry season, hot summer and generally mild winter temperatures. This weather varies somewhat from region to region, giving a subtropical Mediterranean climate with mild winters and long hot summers characteristic of the eastern coast, with an ocean climate of mild rainy winters and long summers of moderate temperature in general in the westernmost part of the province (Cortés de la Frontera and the Guadiaro valley). Málaga´s history as a city goes back over thirty centuries. The Phoenicians were the first to raise a city here alongside an ancient Iberian settlement. Nearby the Greeks later founded Mainake, a centre with trading contact with the Tartessians which eventually was invaded and razed by the Carthaginians. By 205 A.D. the city was allied to Rome and eventually became a Roman Municipality under the Emperor Vespatian. Roman rule did not affect the commercial activity of the city. Exterior commerce was based on the export of oils, cereals, wood, raisins, salted fish, wine and even slaves, and a strong trading based capitalism developed under the control of Jews and Syrians. Around 570 A.D. the city was conquered from the Byzantines by the Visigoths under Leovigildo. The Jews and the Hispano-Romans continued their commercial relations with Italy, Greece and countries in Asia Minor and Africa. In 711 A.D. the Arab conquerors arrived, introducing agricultural techniques and crops up till then unknown in this region. Abd-al-Aziz took charge of the city between

Roman Theatre

714 and 716 and during the Caliphate it became one of the 21 *khoras*, or territorial circumscriptions into which the Kingdom of Al-Andalus was divided. During this time the city became very prosperous, the population numbering as many as 15,000 at the end of the 10th c., with a bourgeois class formed mainly by Jews and *muladies* (Christian converts to Islam). After the first Taifa kingdoms the regions belonging to the moslem Almorávids and Almohades became part of the kingdom of Granada and Málaga became the principal port of this kingdom. For various centuries, two cultures, Christian and Moslem, lived together in harmony. When the conquering Catholic monarchs entered the city in 1487 to incorporate this into the Kingdom of Castile, Málaga formed part of the Nasrid kingdom of Granada, and thus suffered its same fate. The centuries following its inclusion in the kingdom of Castile proved to be a time of decadence, made worse by natural disasters, epidemics, catastrophes and poor harvests. An economic renewal came about in the 19th c. when a notable mercantile and industrial activity began, with the establishment of sugar refineries, textile and tobacco factories, wine cellars and boatyards and even the first steel foundries. But this new prosperity also faded and the first decades of the 20th c. saw Málaga province as one of the most depressed areas of Spain. Fortunately the situation would change later in the same century, with the advent of a new industry which came on the scene in the fifties, tourism.

La Malagueta Beach

La Malagueta Beach

The Alcazaba

The Alcazaba and the Gibralfaro castle together make up the most outstanding monument to Moslem times in Málaga. The Arab presence dates back to 711 A.D., following the invasions of Vandals and Visigoths; the Hammudis, evicted from the Granada kingdoms in 1031 by the Ziries under King Badis, settled in Málaga in 1057 giving impulse to the development of the city.

To the North of the Park lie the gardens of Puerta Oscura and the Alcazaba, one of the few witnesses to Moslem times remaining

The Alcazaba, Málaga

The Alcazaba, Málaga

The Alcazaba, Málaga

in Málaga, built on Roman ruins and dating from the 11th c (1057-1063). This is a fortified enclosure, a reconstruction by the Taifa king Badis el Ziri towards the middle of the 11th c. The palace area is from Nasrid times, the 13th and 14th centuries. The Arab kings from Granada remodelled and amplified this again in the 14th c. It has a double wall with numerous defence towers and twisting entrances for difficult access. Notable among its beautiful gates are the arch of Christ and the arches of Granada, leading to the residential area, with three parallel mansions similar in build to the Alhambra of Granada . This is a very important legacy from Arab times and has been declared a national monument. Inside is the Archaeological museum.

The Alcazaba, Málaga

Roman Theatre

To the west, at the foot of the Alcazaba, lie the remains of a 1ˢᵗ c Roman theatre, built under the Emperor Augustus and in use till the 3rd c. Later, the Arab builders used it as a source of stone for reconstruction of the Alcazaba, hence its present day state of deterioration.

Roman Theatre. Alcazaba

Gibralfaro castle

On the top of the hill we can see the ancient castle of Gibralfaro, joined to the Alcazaba by a walled-in pathway. The origins of this building are lost in the mists of time, since already in Roman times there was a lighthouse, which the Arabs later gave the name *Jabal-Faruk*, meaning "mountain of the lighthouse".

Rebuilt several times under moslem rule, today few elements of the original building remain. From here there is an excellent panoramic view over the city.

Gibralfaro castle

Gibralfaro castle

Alcazaba. Gibralfaro castle

City walls Gibralfaro castle

The Cathedral

The Reconquest of present-day Málaga province took place in the 15th c., between 1485 and 1487.

Cathedral

Then gradual remodelling of the cities was undertaken to adapt these to a different way of living to that of Moslem times.

The first concern of the Catholic monarchs was to repair the city walls, a problem which continued to be of prime importance throughout the 16th c. due to the uprising of the *moriscos* (Christian Moors) and the threat of pirates. The walled perimeter was the original Arab, repairs were limited to only those urgently needed to main an effective defence of the cities won from the Moors. As was their custom, the Catholic Monarchs, on conquering the city, ordered the Mosque to be blessed and consecrated to Christian worship, dedicating this to Santa María de la Encarnación.

In 1488 Cardinal Mendoza commenced building of the Málaga Cathedral

Cathedral

Interior of the Cathedral

Cathedral Facade, the most representative example of Málaga Baroque

under powers given to him by Pope Innocent VIII in the 1486 Bull. The Mosque, built on a wide rectangular base, underwent a series of reforms to adapt it to Christian worship. As the temple turned out to be insufficient for the town's needs, a new Cathedral was proposed in 1528.

The Toledan Enrique Egas was called for, together with the stone quarrier Pedro López, to go over the plans and given their agreement. We do not know for sure who drew up these plans originally, probably Egas himself, Siloé, Hernán Ruíz, or Juan Bautista de Toledo.

The site chosen by Egas and Pedro López was densely built on, requiring some houses to be demolished as work progressed. That same year,1528, foundations

Nuestra Señora de las Angustias, la Piedad

were laid without touching the Mosque so that worship would not be interrupted.

There was confusion in the first stages and in 1541 building was stopped because of errors of calculation. In 1550 the new building, clearly influenced by Diego de Siloé, was started, though we cannot be sure if this latter drew up the model of the head piece.

Interior of the Cathedral, Central nave

Choir stalls in the Cathedral ——

The headpiece and transept wings were finished in the 16th c., in 1587 the Main chapel was covered and decorated, the flooring of red marble from Torcal, and white from Mijas was laid, scaffolding and arch supports removed, and the work stopped, to the disappointment of the Counciller who wanted to carry on. The Cathedral was solemnly consecrated the next year.

The new work was of Renaissance style, with numerous Manierist features which would influence the continuation of Baroque style. Materials are all quarried

Main altar

Cathedral organ, Aldehuela 1779-81

Choir stalls. Pedro de Mena

stone, marbles and jaspers from the province. There are three naves separated by half-point arches on slender cruxiform pillars with joined half columns and classic style cornice and frieze, and above this a second floor of high pillars with inset slender pillars on which the vaults rest.

The lateral naves are the same height as the centre one, typical of the 16th c style which had replaced the terraced Gothic style. On the abside nave *(girola)* are seven rectangular chapels with

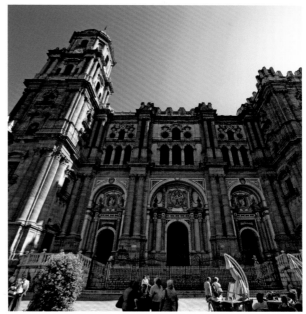

Catedral de Málaga

Choir stalls. Pedro de Mena

triangular buttresses, each hollowed to admit a small sacristy.

For the realization of the Cathedral Choir (1633 -78) many types of woods (mahogany, cedar and pomegranate) were used.

The protagonist of this ambitious work was Pedro de Mena, who left his creative stamp on the choir stalls. Two years was the time allotted for creating the 40 statues of the Saints, a short time which he was able to comply with, however this inevitably affected the quality of the group because part of the work had to be done by the workshop. Years later two new figures (San Blas and San Julián) were ordered, which Mena carved from cedarwood, making a total of 42 figures,

Bishop's palace

the group being completed by 1680. The sculptor has given expressions of great communicative value to the faces of this choirstall, which is one of the most important of Baroque hagiographic galleries. The forms and the technique used are a lasting lesson from the Málaga school, being ideal models for the faithful in their religious practice.

Economic conditions of the council of Málaga at the beginning of the 18th c permitted recommencement of the building of the Cathedral in 1719. Work began on the facade and at the same time on the related towers which together form a solid whole joined by the facie. In 1753 the closure of the Renaissance style vaults commenced, and in 1768 some work was also carried out on the Atrium and the continuation of the towers, only one of which was completed by 1779; most decoration and furnishing was that needed to complete the part of the temple design which related to the temple rites and Masses, the framework of the organs being actual altarpieces in Rococo design and classic form, and in perfect balance with the monumental style of the Cathedral. By 1783, however, with no hope of being able to continue because of the withdrawal of sponsorship, the scaffolding of the towers was taken down and work declared finished. In 1796 a further attempt to carry on was made, but the works had by now been definitely paralysed.

Church of the Sacristy. 15th - 18th

Church of the Sacristy

19

Church de los Mártires. 15th - 18th

Church de los Mártires

Church of the Sagrado Corazón

Municipal Foundation Pablo Ruíz Picasso. Museum "Casa Natal"

The Fundación Pablo Ruíz Picasso Museo Casa Natal (Museum at the home where Picasso was born on 25th October 1881 and part of the Picasso Foundation) was established 26th February 1988 as an autonomous body under Municipal

Plaza de la Merced

agreement, occupying the first floor of the building from 1988 to 1997.

In 1991 it was made part of the Spanish Museums system. After it was reformed and extended to occupy to the rest of the building, official inauguration by King Juan Carlos and Queen Sofia took place on 22nd June 1998.

Picasso

Museum interior

Museum Casa Natal Picasso

The Museum is situated in the historial centre of Málaga, an area of architectural style typical of the 19th c., comprising the Plaza de la Merced, the other Picasso Museum, the Parish of Santiago, the Alcazaba and the Municipal Theatre of Miguel de Cervantes.

From 1880 to 1883 the first floor of this house was rented by José Ruíz Blasco, father of the artist, who later moved to the 3rd floor of No. 32 of the same Plaza. On being named Art teacher in La Coruña in 1891, he moved to this Galician city where the family stayed until 1895.

The ground floor has exhibits related to Picasso and his cultural and living surroundings; the museum of the first floor has works by the artist and some by his father, Jose Ruíz Blasco, as well as memorabilia of Picasso and his family.

On the other floor there is a library and document centre with diverse material to facilitate further study of the artist and his works.

Picasso was baptized in the Santiago Parish, one of the oldest of Málaga, with its Baroque interior and *mudéjar* (Arab) tower. His paternal grandparents had married here, and his parents, in 1880; his sisters, Dolores and Concepción were also baptized here.

Picasso's first playgound, and where he may have made his first drawings, was the Plaza de la Merced. In the 15th c. it had been a public marketplace; it was a leisure area for the bourgeois at the end of the 19th c, the bells of the Church of the Merced alongside Picasso's house bearing witness to a many hued variety of people who would in time be reflected in works of this genius.

Calle Granada

Centre nave of Santiago

Museo Picasso Málaga

The main aim of the new Museum was to make one of Picasso´s dreams come true, that of having his own museum in his birthplace town. Not only to emphasize the origin and the Andalusian spirit of this genius but to bring his cosmopolitan creations to his Andalusian homeground where the innovating spirit of surely the most outstanding creator of plastic art of the 20th century might serve as example to future generations. Thus, alongside the permanent collection on display is an ambitious plan for temporary and varied exhibitions which will reflect the varied themes and aspects of Picasso's world and that of his contemporaries. An original and orientative guide for getting better acquainted with his works, which cover at least three quarters of the 20th c.

Picasso Museum Málaga

Picasso Museum Málaga

Interior patio

23

Picasso Museum, Málaga

To house the collection and as location for the Museum, the Andalusian Council purchased the mansion Palacio de los Condes de Buenavista, an historic building typical of Andalusian civil architecture of the 16th c., with mixed Renaissance and Mudéjar (Arab) features. Moreover, apart from its undisputable historic and artistic interest, this building is strategically situated in the very centre of the city's historic nucleus, and the Palace of Buenavista itself was declared a National Monument in 1939.

However, that a historic building should come back to life with a redefined function, does not mean there were no problems and difficulties, often quite unexpected. What was clear at first was that the reform had to go beyond the space available to the the Palacio de Buenavista if the new Institution were to enjoy such services necessary to museumography, as library, documentary centre, auditorium and educative department and offices, etc. Those of both foundations responsible considered indispensable that many areas adjacent to the Palacio should be acquired, and where, once they had been adapted and integrated, these services and functions would be put. Additionally this amplification would act to increase the value of the surrounding ancient mediaeval town centre being preserved, thus protecting this from further degradation. Here a series of new buildings of modern design have been built, holding temporary exhibitions, a restoration workshop, the bookshop and some offices. With these new areas added, the total surface area of the Málaga Picasso Museum will total some 8,300

Picasso Museum, Málaga

Picasso Museum, Málaga

Picasso Museum, Málaga

sq. metres. When test boring underneath the Palacio an unexpected discovery of remains from the Phoenician, Roman and Nasrid cultures was made. It was decided at once to complete the excavation with great care, study these ruins and not only leave them intact but integrate them in a new plan for the building, so that they might be seen by the public, together with the works of Picasso; this effort made even more splendidly obvious the rich cultural character of Málaga, as it once was and still is, centuries later.

The Park, Málaga

Málaga Capital

The Municipal Town House was built between 1912 and 1919: of neoBaroque style, it has a rectangular base and four wings around a centre patio. The main wing has a centred portico on a terraced plinth, above which there is a large a public address balcony and fascie. The exterior decoration is of great interest, with its slender pillars joined to the walls and numerous columns and windows.

Málaga Town house

Málaga Town house

On the front there is a large tympanum in classic style with carvings, work of the sculptor Francisco Palma, which shows a matronly figure, symbolizing Málaga, surrounded by allegorical figures representing architecture, the sea, fishing and trade. As usual

in this type of official building, the whole is crowned by an ornate clocktower. The other facades have been decorated with a style giving the impression of movement with figures placed in different depth positioning. The interior of the Town house has a sumptuous stairway, imperial in design, with Italian marble handrails, stained glass windows, mirrors, paintings

The Cenachero

Museum of Malaga. Customs Palace

Marques de Larios

and many other works of art. The Chapter hall (Salon de Sesiones) holds a copy of the Lex Flavia Malacitana, a decree by the Emperor Domitian between 81 and 94 a.D.

The present layout of the port dates from the 19th c, but technical changes in recent times have revolutionized transport and the port has embarked on an ample plan for remodellation which will eventually extend its ground area to double that of the original. The Queen Mary 2, largest and most exclusive passenger ship in the world, visited Málaga on its maiden voyage in 2004.

Málaga Town house

Málaga is situated on the coast, on the banks of the Guadalmedina River which divides the city in two. On arriving at the centre, we can see the port and alongside this, a magic tropical garden, our fascinating Parque, set out in the 19th c. on land reclaimed from the sea. Málaga city has 16 beautiful beaches, those to the East are: La Malagueta, La Caleta, Baños

Interior of Art and folklore museum

Málaga Port, the "Queen Mary 2"

Málaga Park . Port

Málaga Park

Palacio de Miramar

Centre of Contemporary art

Municipal Museum, Málaga

del Carmen, Pedregalejo-Las Acacias, El Palo, El Chanquete, El Candado, El Peñon del Cuervo, Fábrica de Cemento and La Araña. Those to the West are: Huelin, San Andrés, La Misericordia, Guadalmar, Guadalhorce, and Campo de Golf. All these are beaches with moderate waves and a high rate of occupation; most have a sea promenade and are situated within the urban area.

Beach La Malagueta Sea promenade, Paseo Marítimo Pablo Ruíz Picasso

Lighthouse

La Malagueta looking west

Beach at Pedregalejo

Sardines on skewers

The Sanctuary (Santuario) Nuestra Señora de la Victoria is situated where the Catholic Monarchs camped during the seige of Málaga in 1487. Here Our Lady of Victory is worshipped, the oldest Patron of the City, ceded to Málaga by the Monarchs after the conquest. The present day church was inaugurated in 1700. It has a Latincross base, with Main Altar and box tower which has at its foot the pantheon-crypt of the noble Buenavista family, with one of the most lugubrious funereal atmospheres to be seen in Spanish crypts.

Nuestra Señora de la Victoria Sanctuary

Santa María de la Victoria

Central Nave

Pantheon of the Condes de Buenavista

Cervantes Theatre

Cervantes Theatre

Museo Carmen Thyssen

Echegaray Theatre

Málaga Port

During the last third of the 19th c., the Restauración and Antonio Canovas de Castillo, its great Spanish political arbiter, had a great impact on Málaga. At that time, the seawaters of the bay came right up to the foot of the Customs house, which meant that the sea reached the city limits with no natural barrier save the streets themselves.

The Royal Decree of 5th September 1896 ordered the filling in of a large part of the port; at first the consequences of this iniciative and what this would mean to Málaga were not fully appreciated, but as the immense size of the newly reclaimed part between the Hospital Noble and the Plaza de la Marina became apparent, people realized that something very important was taking place, on a par with the inauguration of the Calle Larios five years previously.

Calle Larios

Plaza de la Constitución

Easter week: Semana Santa

Málaga's **Fair** has its origins in 1491, after Málaga was incorporated into the Kingdom of Castile. It starts on Friday of the week before the 19th August and for 9 consecutive nights,entertainment and fun fill the streets, the tents and fairground with flowers, lanterns, typical flamenco and other dresses, *malagueña* and *sevillana* dances and the elegant promenading of horse and carriage.

The Fair also spreads outside the fairgrounds: the Romeria (pilgrimage) the bullfights in the Malagueta, the music festivales in the Cervantes Theatre, regattas in the port. The Málaga fair in August, the *feria,* is the great summer fair, open, cosmopolitan and international, reflecting the character of the capital of the top tourist area in Europe, the Costa del Sol. Music plays a fundamental part in each of the acts to enjoy in the streets and squares of Málaga: the *Verdiales* (Málaga folkmusic) in Calle Larios, or the International Folklore Festival in the Plaza de la Marina. Gastronomy, too, is an important feature and we can accompany our enjoyment with the generous local wines.

Thousands of people fill the streets of the Historic centre, later they can attend the bullfights in the Malagueta bullring. This bullfighting celebration is one of the most important in Spain. In the same ring, the annual horse and carriage show called *Ciudad de Málaga,* is held on Saturday evening of the Fair.

Bullring at the Malagueta. Málaga Fair

Bullring at the Malagueta

Málaga Fair

Congress Hall Palacio de Ferias y Congresos, Málaga

San Andrés Beach, Paseo Maritimo Antonio Machado

La Concepción Historic Botanical Garden

Six km. from the city lies the Finca de la Concepción, the most beautiful and important tropical garden in Spain and one of the best of all Europe. The gardens hold many exotic plants and trees, some from Africa, Asia and Australia.

It is a garden to be admired at any time of the year since the gardens hold mainly tropical and perennial plants: amazing Ficus, splendid Araucaria-the Norfolk Pine, tall elegant palms, a giant Dragon tree from the Canary Islands, strange cycas and giant Strelitzia, "Birds of Paradise".

Exhuberent flowering vine all over the Gardens   *Mirador*

The Nymph's pond   *Small ironwork bridge*

Western Costa del Sol

The Costa del Sol is that part of the Andalusian coast which goes from Manilva to Nerja: a nearly uninterrupted coastline "road" of over 90 kilometres, lined with hotels, urbanizations, towns, beaches and peaceful bays, golf courses and tennis courts, casinos and nautical clubs. This is the famous west Costa del Sol, known as the beach of Europe.

Its thousand-year history has made it one of the most important cultural-tourist centres of western Europe, legacy of the many different invading peoples who have reached its coasts. Málaga no longer exports raisins, almonds or wine as before, instead, it is now the centre of an economic re-birth, the sun being its main commodity.

The climate is typically Mediterranean, with mild winters, hot summers and very little rain. The mean annual temperature is 18 deg. C. The peaceful warm-watered Mediterranean acts as a thermostat, and it is no exaggeration to state that Málaga enjoys a year round Spring, this being one of its main attractions.

The Costa del Sol is known all over the world as being one of the most important tourist centres. The first impression the visitor receives is the ample range of entertainments on offer: the sea in all its varied aspects, nautical and sport installations, restaurants, discoteques and shows and its exceptional offer of over 40 golf courses, which have given it its other name of the "Costa del Golf"- yet underneath the neon of modern day, the Costa del Sol retains those virtues which charmed the earliest visitors: clean uncontaminated air, seas of blue warm waters and a great spread of beaches, bays, cliffs in beautiful contrast against a backdrop of hills.

Torremolinos

Torremolinos

Originally a primitive milling and fisherman's village, this was where the Costa del Sol and the Málaga tourist boom was born in the fifties, at 12 km from the capital and 7 km only from the international airport. Torremolinos grew up in the 19th c., a group of houses around the towers and mills of the zone. Today the mills have disappeared, leaving their name to hotels, roads and byways. La Carihuela, old fishing area, is the best place to savour the world famous Málaga dish; *pescaito frito*, or *fritura malagueña* – mixed fried fish.

Torremolinos

Playa de la Carihuela. Torremolinos

Torremolinos

San Miguel street, Torremolinos

Playa de la Carihuela. Torremolinos

39

Benalmádena

Benalmádena is a coastal town with backdrop of mountains, in three distinct parts: Benalmádena Pueblo with its typical Andalusian architecture of white houses and balconies full of flowers. The Jardines del Muro (Wall Gardens) were designed by Cesar Manrique. Arroyo de la Miel is the most populated, here the flamenco shows, disco-theques, snacks (tapas), good seafood and fried fish delight the visitor. It also has magnificent sports installations. Finally, Benalmádena Costa, which has 9 km of beachfront with warm calm waters and one of the most important Sports marinas in Spain.

Statue Niña de Benalmádena

Plaza. Benalmádena Pueblo

Benalmádena Pueblo

Church of Benalmádena

Benalmádena Pueblo

Beach at Benalmádena

Beach at Benalmádena

Sport Marina, Benalmádena

Golf course

Bil-Bil Castle, Benalmádena Costa

Benalmádena Costa

Fuengirola.

Is a coastal town spreading out to Carvajal and Los Boliches. The many signs of Phoenician, Arab and Roman cultures prove that through the ages, this privileged place captivated all who came here. Known as Seul to the Romans, it was Sohail to the Arabs, who under Abderraman III built the castle here with that name; the ruins still can be seen on the hill. On the sea promenade, the longest of the Costa del Sol, stands the facade of a Roman temple which was never completed.

Monument to Our Lady of Carmen

In spite of the great advances in tourist infrastructure, Fuengirola has maintained its Andalusian character and kept its traditions alive.

The mildness of its semitropical climate and its 8 km. of wonderful and well-kept beaches of fine sand, with all services and a magnificent promenade, the *Paseo*

Fuengirola, Seafront promenade

Marítimo, have made this a central point for a variety of excursions and the practice of all kinds of tourism: Nature walks, studies of Culture and History, Rural Tourism, etc.

The fisherman's area of Los Boliches has wide beaches and there are many families here traditionally dedicated to work at sea; on offer to visitors and residents in its many typical restaurants and *chiringuitos* are fried fish, baked fish or sardines on skewers. There are many reasons why so many Spaniards and other Europeans have chosen this as their new home.

Beaches on the west of Fuengirola

Fishing and sports port, Fuengirola

Beach, Fuengirola

Fuengirola

Beaches at Fuengirola

Fuengirola

Mijas

The mountain range of Mijas is known as the "lungs of the Costa del Sol" for its dense pine groves among which lies the white limewashed town of Mijas. From the town we can see the whole Costa and even the mountains of Northern Africa. The town itself reflects the classic Arab design of narrow streets and white walls. Mijas has become a haven for artists and foreigners, all attracted by its picturesque aspect and the beauty of the countryside which surrounds it.

Partial view , Mijas Pueblo *Golf course*

Mijas pueblo, Main square

Typical street in Mijas

Bullring, Mijas

Donkey taxis, Mijas

Typical street in Mijas

Mijas Pueblo

Marbella

Is situated at the foot of the Sierra Blanca, on the old Via Augusta, the road which once joined Rome with Tartessus; the old town is partly surrounded by walls and an Arab castle; here there is an old Roman bridge over the River Nagüelles. The Town house dates from the 16th c, as do the Bazán hospital, the convents of San Francisco and La Trinidad and the hospital of San Juan de Dios. We know that Cervantes, author of Don Quixote, once stayed in the Convent of San Francisco mill, now in ruins.

The layout of the town is typically Andalusian, with narrow streets and whitewashed houses, contrasting with the tourist blocks of the seventies and

Castle and city walls, Marbella

Santa María de la Encarnación, 18th c

Plaza de los Naranjos

Panoramic view of the city, promenade

Los Monteros Golf Course, Marbella

Puerto Banús beaches

Avenida del Mar

Paseo Marítimo promenade

La Fontanilla beach

Mosque, Marbella

Estepona, seafront promenade

Estepona

Typical Andalusian architecture, Puerto Banús, Marbella

Puerto Banús. Marbella

Manilva. Puerto de la Duquesa

Ojén   *Casares*

eighties, the modern installations and residential areas. There are three ports for nautical sports (one being the famous Puerto Banús) and ample sports facilities on offer, among which are many golf courses.

Marbella is today one of the most important tourist centres of Spain. Nature has also had a hand in accentuating the attractiveness and character of Marbella, offering a mild climate, varied scenery, skies nearly always clear, fresh and blue, and an abundance of natural riches.

Gaucín

San Pedro de Alcántara is one of the Costa's population nuclei, a national centre of tourist interest, with ruins of the Roman colony of Silniana, containing valuable mosaics, and the thermal baths of La Bóveda. In Linda Vista there are remains of the Paleo-Christian basilica of Vega del Mar, necropolis of the Visigoths.

Estepona, of Roman origin and set in the Sierra Bermeja, has retained its typical fishing and farming areas.

Lying between Gibraltar and Marbella, is has a warm microclimate and mean annual temperatures of 18,5 deg C. There are over 325 days of sunshine a year, with winds predominating from the west and east.

In this beautiful town the bright blue of the sea contrasts with the white streets and colourful flowers under a kindly sun. From its magnificent beaches of fine sand we can see to the west the singular silhouette of the Rock of Gibraltar.

Ronda and its Serranía

That part of the Malaga region which starts from the capital and goes towards the west, following the bends of the Guadalhorce river, can be considered the most pure example of the essence of Andalusia. The groves of holm-oaks, pines and Spanish firs of the *serranía* (mountains) of Ronda were once home to the *bandoleros* (highwaymen), not only the famed José María el Tempranillo, or Pasos Largos, in the 18th and 19th centuries, but right from times of the Caliphate of Corboba, when the rebel Omar Ben Hafsun established his centre of operations in Bobastro.

Ronda, at an altitude of 750m, is the capital of the Serranía. This thousand year old city has enjoys an important artistic and historic wealth. A gorge 150m deep divides the town in 2 parts, the La Ciudad and El Mercadillo, joined by a stonework bridge from the 18th c. The first area has kept its traditional flavour of narrow streets, barred windows, old mansions and churches,

Ruins of the Roman Theatre of Acinipo

Monument to Cayetano Ordoñez. Ronda

Panoramic view of the Tajo de Ronda

Puerta de Felipe V. Puente Viejo

impressive witness to its rich past. El Mercadillo on the other side of the Puente Nuevo bridge, is the administrative and commercial centre though it too has outstanding old buildings and churches. The new bridge, Puente Nuevo, New Bridge, was built between 1735 and 1793, so called as it replaces one that sank into the abyss. The bridge has three openings, the centre one made up of two superimposed arches. The two closed side parts were once used as prisons. The bridge is 98 m high. Ronda should be visited with time and patience, so its many monuments, beautiful corners and the details of its typical architecture can be appreciated. We should not miss the famous La Maestranza de Ronda bullring, relic of bullfighting built in 1785 by Martín de Aldehuela; the terraces and two galleries of low arches are of stone, the entrance portal in neoclassic style with Baroque adornment. The 16th c. Puerta de Carlos V, the *mudejar* style minaret of San Sebastián, the Espíritu Santo church built in the reign of the Catholic Monarchs Isabella and Ferdinand, the Santa María La Mayor church, built over an old mosque, and the elegant facade of the Marqués de Salvatierra mansion from the 18th c. are other sights to see. Alongside the river are the remaining three rooms of the Arab thermal baths, and 10 km from Ronda we can visit the ruins and the Roman Theatre of Acinipo, known as Ronda la Vieja.

Church of Santa María la Mayor

Interior patio, Palacio de Mondragón

Church of Santa María la Mayor

Panorama of the walls of Ronda

Arab baths, 13th c

Bullring of Ronda, from 1785, called the bullfighter's sanctuary

City of Ronda

Guadalhorce valley, Antequera

The Fuente de Piedra Lagoon, an ecological protected area with a water surface of 1,300 hectares, lying near the town of the same name, is a salt water lake with no natural outlet. The lake and its surroundings form the major breeding ground for flamingos in all Europe. The Peñon de los Enamorados *(Lover's cliff)* is a mountain of Jurassic limestone, 874 m high, between the towns of Archidona and Antequera, a sheer mass standing out on the plain evoking the embrace of two lovers. The story goes that two lovers, she Arab and he Christian, and for this reason not able to marry, chose to throw themselves into the abyss to avoid

Laguna de Fuente de Piedra

Antequera castle

being caught and forced to renounce their love. There is a painting in the Town House of Malaga which refers to this legend.

Just 13 km. from Antequera on the road to Malaga, is the Torcal range of mountains, an amazing sight where natural forces have modelled the landscape, creating a bizarre city of rocks evoking figures and monuments of great beauty. The huge blocks of limestone have been eroded in a characteristic Karst formations, creating such fantasies as the Molar, the Eagle, the Screw, the Lizard, etc. The rock

Antequera

called the Seven Tables makes a wonderful lookout point from which one can see the whole rugged surface of the higher Torcal. Antequera lies on an important crossroad between the Guadalquivir Valley, the plains of Granada and the Mediterranean coast. The thousand-year old Antequera has been a thoroughfare of the different primitive communities since the first settled in the Iberian Peninsular in the Mid- Paleolithic. It is

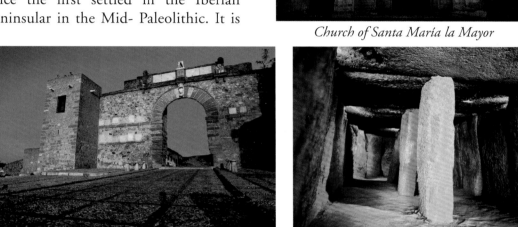

Church of Santa María la Mayor

Antequera, Giant's arch

Interior of Dolmen at Menga

from the Bronze Age however, that most of the important prehistoric remains here have come, such as the Dolmen groups of Menga, Viera and El Romeral, dating from 2500 to 2000 B.C. Witness to our prehistory is Menga, the most splendid and well preserved of the Calcolithic age dolmens. This consists of a large oval hall, a covered gallery with a narrow entrance; it has seven huge square monoliths on each side, above which an enormous flat slab with five large flagstones make up the roof. This is the only one of the three dolmens which contains carved inscriptions, representing anthromorphic figures, to be seen on the first stone on the left of the entrance and estimated to be some 4,500 years old.

Eastern Costa del Sol, Axarquia

That part of the Malaga Province between the capital and the border with Granada province has two names, defining two separate areas: the eastern Costa del Sol along the sea, and Axarquia inland. Axarquia bears the quintessential stamp of Malaga's Moslem ages, with its small pueblos crowning the mountains and joined by zigzagging roads. This area produces the raisins *(pasas)* which made Malaga famous. Velez-Malaga, capital of the Axarquia, lies halfway between the coast

and the mountains, in a hollow alongside of the Velez river. The presence of the Phoenicians, Carthaginians and Romans in succession has bequeathed the urban centre of Velez-Málaga a richly varied monumental wealth.

Torre del Mar

Golf course

Cómpeta

Velez-Malaga castle

58 Drying raisins under the sun to make pasas

Frigiliana

A few kilometres from Nerja lies the picturesque mountainside villa of Frigiliana with its whitewashed houses, an idyllic reflection of the Andalusian pueblo. Its handcrafts, of all types, are highly valued for their extraordinary quality. Nearby we also have the lovely pueblo of Cómpeta, famed for its sweet wines and quality raisins.

According to legend, it is in **Torrox** that Abderramán settled after disembarking in Almuñecar. Under Moslem rule this was a manufacturing centre for silks, which then were exported to Damascus and Baghdad. A visit to the nearby Convent of Las Nieves is well worth our while. The beaches at Torrox are lined with important tourist installations.

General view of Frigiliana

Typical Morisco Street

Frigiliana

Torrox Costa

Nerja

The most eastern of the Costa del Sol towns, Nerja is a well known residential and summer centre; it has an impressive mirador to offer the tourist, built on the remains of an old fortress, and known as the Balcón de Europe. This is a on high rocky extension overlooking the sea, with the rugged peaks of the Sierra de Almijara behind the town. Nerja has been inhabited since prehistoric times, as witnessed by the cave paintings discovered in the grottos of the famous Nerja Caves. It was at its most splendid in times of the Moslems, when it was known as Narixa, meaning "abundant fountains". The streets of Nerja have maintained their original tracing. A visit to the Virgen de las Angustias and the church of San Salvador, from the 17th and 18th c. is recommended.

Paseo del Balcón de Europa

Plaza de Nerja

Calahonda beach

Burriana beach

La Caletilla Beach, Nerja

Nerja Caves

Beach at Maro

Plentiful variety of foods, Paella

Burriana beach, Nerja

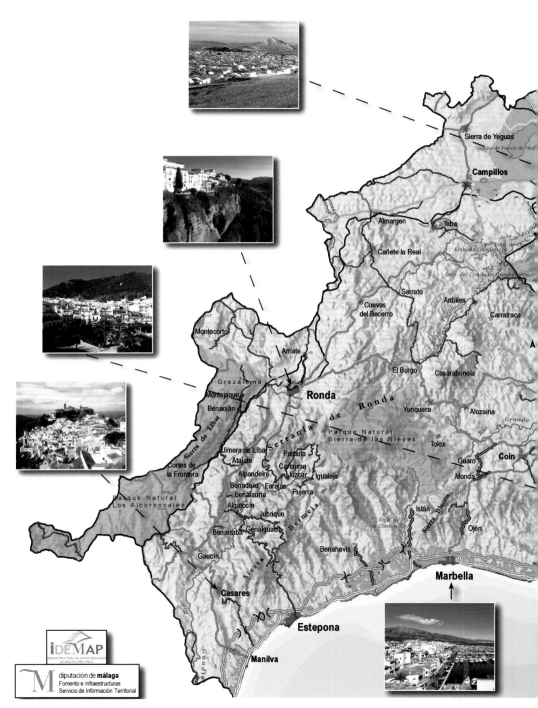

Sierra de Yeguas

Laguna de Fuente de Pied

Campillos

Almargen

Teba

Cañete la Real

Emb. de Guada
Emb. del Guadalepe

Emb. del Conde de Guadalorce

Serrato

Ardales

Carratraca

Cuevas
del Becerro

Á

Montecorto

El Burgo

Casarabonela

Arriate

Grazalema

Ronda

Montejaque

Benaoján

Serrania de Ronda

Yunquera

Alozaina

Grande

Sierra de Líbar

Parque Natural
Sierra de las Nieves

Tolox

Jimera de Líbar

Parauta

Atajate

Cartajima

Río

Cortes de
la Frontera

Alpandeire

Júzcar

Igualeja

Guaro

Coín

Benadalid   Faraján

Pujerra

Monda

Benalauria

Algatocín

Istán

Sierra Blanca

Parque Natural
Los Alcornocales

Jubrique

Sierra Bermeja

Emb. de
la Concepción

Ojén

Benarrabá

Genalguacil

Gaucín

Benahavís

Marbella

Casares

Estepona

Manilva

IDEMAP
INFRAESTRUCTURA DE DATOS ESPACIALES
DE MÁLAGA PROVINCIA

M diputación de málaga
Fomento e Infraestructuras
Servicio de Información Territorial

62

Alameda

Cuevas
de San Marcos

Cuevas Bajas

Villanueva
de Algaidas

Villanueva
de Tapia

Mollina

Laguna de
Herrera

Archidona

Río

Guadalhorce

España

MÁLAGA
Costa del Sol

tequera

Sierra

del

Torcal

de Abdalajis

Villanueva de la
Concepción

Villanueva del Trabuco

Villanueva
del Rosario

Alfarnate

Alfarnatejo

Riogordo

Periana

Sierra

Casabermeja

Colmenar

Embalse de
la Viñuela

Alcaucín

Canillas de Aceituno

Tejeda

Parque Natural
Montes de Málaga

Cómares

Viñuela

Sedella

Salares

Canillas de Albaida

Sierra

Almogía

Montes de Málaga

Cútar

Benamargosa

Árchez

Cómpeta

Almáchar

El Borge

Arenas

Parque Natural Sierra
Tejeda, Almijara

Almijara

Benamocarra

Vélez-Málaga

Moclinejo

Sayalonga

Frigiliana

Totalán

Iznate

Macharaviaya

Algarrobo

Torrox

Vélez

Nerja

Cártama

MÁLAGA

Rincón de la Victoria

Alhaurín de la Torre

rín el Grande
e Mijas

Torremolinos

Benalmádena

Fuengirola

MAR
MEDITERRÁNEO

63

INDEX